Chicago Blues Guitar

by Artie Traum
and Arti Funaro

Oak Publications
New York · London · Sydney

Oak Publications has conducted an exhaustive search to locate the composers, publishers, or copyright owners of the compositions in this book. However, in the event that we have inadvertently published a previously copyrighted composition without proper acknowledgement, we advise the copyright owner to contact us so that we may give appropriate credit in future editions.

Book design by Nina Clayton
Cover by Tim Metevier
Front and back cover photos by Ray Flerlage
Edited by Peter Pickow and Brooke Hedick

Photo Credits:
pages 6, 15, 35, 56, 69, 72, 77, 92 and 94: D. Shigley
page 62: Marc PoKempner
page 80: Amy O'Neal/Living Blues Magazine
page 88: Courtesy Homesick James Williamson/Living Blues Magazine

© 1983 Oak Publications
A Division of Embassy Music Corporation, New York
All Rights Reserved

US ISBN 0.8256.0241.6
UK ISBN 0.7119.0387.5

Distributed throughout the world by Music Sales Corporation:
799 Broadway, New York N.Y. 10003 USA
78 Newman Street, London W1P 3LA England
27 Clarendon Street, Artarmon, Sydney NSW 2064 Australia

Printed in the United States of America by
Vicks Lithograph and Printing Corporation
8/83

CONTENTS

Preface 5
Introduction 7
   A Word on Guitars 11
   Basic Tablature and How To Use It 13
   Bends, Vibrato, and Tremolo 16
   To Pick or Not to Pick 18
Twelve-Bar Blues 21
The Shuffle Lick 26
Blues Scales 31
Bottleneck and Slide Guitar 36
   "Wild about You" 41
Riffs 43
   Earl Hooker 43
   Son Seals 46
   Howlin' Wolf/Hubert Sumlin 47
   Otis Rush 48
   Elmore James 50
   Hound Dog Taylor 51
   Albert King 52
   B.B. King 54
Albert King 57
   "Walked All Night Long" 58
   "Natural Ball" 63
   "Crosscut Saw" 66
Muddy Waters 68
   "Long Distance Call" 70
Buddy Guy 73
   "A Man and the Blues" 73
   "Mary Had a Little Lamb" 78
Freddie King 80
   "Dust My Broom" 81
   "I'm Goin' Down" 83
   "Hidden Away" 85
   "Swishy" 89
   "San-Dee-Ay-Go" 90
B.B. King 92
   "I Lost My Thrill" 93
Discography 94
Bibliography 95

PREFACE

A young, cheeky kid, dressed in suburban denim from head to toe, sat in the sweltering basement of New York's Cafe Au Go-Go practicing some bluesy slide-guitar riffs on an old Fender Jazzmaster. The year was 1968, and the Au Go-Go was packed for its bi-annual 'Blues Bag', a nonstop three-day performance that brought together the best blues artists from across America. Mississippi John Hurt, old and frail, fingerpicked gracefully on stage, while other acts warmed up in a crowded, hectic backstage area. Despite the commotion, the kid continued scraping his slide across the strings, shaking his hand until it was a blur along the fretboard.

"That's not how you want to be doin' that," he heard someone say firmly. "You don't want to shake your hand like it's Jello. Do it easy. . .nice and easy."

"You want to make those strings moan," the Wolf said easing the slide off of the kid's pinky. "Like a woman. Try the slide on your third finger too. . .your pinky is too weak to control it. Now try it, go on!"

The kid looked up slowly. His eyes froze, suddenly focusing on the huge form of Howlin' Wolf who suddenly dropped to his knees with a great thud.

The kid couldn't move. He was awed by the presence of this great legend. The Wolf let out a raspy laugh, shook his head, and struggled to his feet.

"Ooooeeeh," he laughed. "You come on out and watch my band. You got a lot to learn."

A few minutes later, the Wolf and his band hit the stage, immediately launching into a steamy version of "Smokestack Lightnin'." The audience came alive, screaming and yelling as the Wolf, sweat pouring off him from all sides, leapt gracefully around the stage. The Wolf's guitarist, young, white, and adept, copied the parts Hubert Sumlin had played on Howlin' Wolf's Chess LPs many years earlier. The Wolf rolled his eyes, fell to the floor, and began his famous moan. The sound blended with the guitar to make an unearthly vibration—all at once sexy, magical, and more than a little bit scary.

Howlin' Wolf captured the best of Chicago blues in his moaning. If anything, it was undeniably infectious, compelling, and shattering. The first time I ever heard it, on record, I was a goner. I craved more. I went out and bought every Chicago-blues style record that was available at the time, seeking the great guitarists, and finding the three Kings: Albert, B.B., and Freddie. Other Chicago artists, confined to playing their music in the funky clubs that lined Chicago's South Side, were simply not available to national audiences at that time. One had to carefully seek out their work. The Blues Revival of the sixties and seventies, aided by the popularity of younger blues-influenced artists like the Rolling Stones, Jimi Hendrix, Canned Heat, the Blues Project, and others, certainly helped to bring more obscure Chicago players into the public eye. Guitarists like Hound Dog Taylor, J.B. Lenoir, Buddy Guy, Otis Rush, and many others enjoyed a brief moment of recognition during those years. This book is a tribute to their soulful genius.

The term 'Chicago blues' may be somewhat inaccurate. Most of the blues guitarists we have studied grew up in the South, developing their styles in Mississippi, Alabama, and Kansas City. They migrated to Chicago after World War II, following other rural blacks who emigrated to the industrial North. Chicago was *the* city that brought the best bluesmen together and it was here that many of them did their best work. If the blues were born in Mississippi, they matured in Chicago, and it was in Chicago that the blues went *electric*. Old Gibson, Martin, and National guitars were replaced by Fender Stratocasters, Gibson Les Pauls, and other electric marvels. The blues became barroom dance music for a generation of black families who were in Chicago seeking better times. Like the town itself, Chicago blues were tough, fierce, and soulful.

This book is a study of the guitar styles of the most prominent, innovative and interesting guitarists who made their names in Chicago. We have chosen to concentrate on B.B. King, Otis Rush, Muddy Waters, Albert King, Elmore James, Freddie King, and others who helped make blues history in Chicago. We would like to apologize for any omissions in this list, since many of the lesser-known names were equally responsible for new, innovative guitar styles.

Chicago is the city we will be looking at, but we have tried to stress the various influences, from jazz to country-and-western, that gave electric blues its depth and character. The blues never die because they can always adapt. The basic form is structured yet fluid with the result that it can be used by a progressive jazz ensemble playing an abstract improvisation as well as by a traditional blues band with equally valid results. The music expresses a basic human condition and, although it took the often suppressed genius of black American culture to expose it, all people seem to respond to its basic truth. Both Arti and I grew up listening to blues, finding in its raw power an alternative to the glossy facade of middle-class white culture. We tried to learn this style of music, admiring the musicians we copied from, knowing that they never had books or records to learn from.

We have often wondered how the blues came into being, and why it chose the route to Chicago to become a fully-realized art form. Obvious causes though they may be, poverty and oppression alone don't explain the blues. These external forces had to mix with an unconscious, creative drive that disrupts the lives of so many artists and drives them half-crazy with the need to create. This was the "Hell-Hound" that snapped at Robert Johnson's restless soul, torturing his all-too-short life. This is the grace that makes Albert King's huge hands gentle, when they bend strings up and down the length of his guitar. This is the moan that rumbled through Howlin' Wolf, the dry, pleading moan that seemed to shake his entire body. When he moved the slide on that kid's finger, in the basement of the Cafe Au Go Go, in 1968, he did it with the authority of a true Master.

"You want those strings to moan," the Wolf had said. "You got a lot to learn...."

ARTIE TRAUM

Howlin' Wolf

INTRODUCTION

> Chicago, Chicago
> That toddlin' town (Toddlin' town)
> Chicago, Chicago
> I'll show you around, I love it!
> "Chicago" by Fred Fisher

> Chicago's tough, Chicago's mean
> Worst old city I've ever seen.
> Old Blues Verse

Boiling hot in the summer, freeezing in the winter, Chicago is a city of extremes. The wealthy live in splendid high-rise apartments overlooking Lake Michigan while the less fortunate crowd into old, crumbling frame-tenements in the city's ghettos. For the rich, the bitter winds that whip across town are at worst a nuisance; at best they're a source of poetic pride about life in the Windy City. For the poor, they are a constant reminder of the harsh realities of urban life—a person can actually freeze to death. One angry blues singer put it this way:

Cold winds make me shiver
Cold wind gets my goat;
I feel so damn disgusted
Ain't got no overcoat.

Muddy Waters often said you had to "lean in and push" in order to survive. Chicago was a natural breeding ground for the blues.

For a while Chicago was the economic center of the country. It was around the turn of the century that it earned its reputation as a corrupt, cutthroat, ruthless, and powerful town. Railroads converged downtown like spokes on a giant wheel where the golden fields of wheat cut in the midwest were packed and shipped out on giant freight trains. Chicago slaughtered the nation's meat—Carl Sandberg called the city 'Hog Butcher To The Nation". Skyscrapers grew downtown, while huge factories, packing plants, lumber yards, and steel mills sprawled across land that once grew wheat, corn, and potatoes.

MOVING NORTH

Thousands of people were drawn to Chicago like ants to honey. The Windy City promised good wages, upward mobility, and big-town excitement. There were many migrations to Chicago, but it was after World War II, when the industrial economy went into overdrive, that thousands of Southern black farmers and sharecroppers left their homes to gamble on a new life in the North. Conditions in the South were so bad that blacks thought there was little to lose and much to gain in Detroit, Cleveland, New York, or Chicago.

While the Mississippi Delta could boast fertile farmland and the mighty Mississippi River, black families living there suffered a grinding and bitter poverty that still exists. During the 1930s a successful sharecropper might earn only 200 to 500 dollars for a year of back-breaking effort. Since sharecropping is an exchange of labor for the use of land, tools, and a percentage of the crop, it keeps most farmers in constant debt to their landowners. As recently as 1959, according to blues historian Pete Welding, "more than 80 percent of Mississippi Negro families were existing on less than $3,000 family income annually." Chicago must have looked awfully good to people living with "poverty, perpetual hunger, poor health and disease, rudimentary educational opportunities, systematically administered brutality, death. . . ." Yet it was this oppressively steaming hot Delta area that produced classic American country blues from 1910 to 1940. It is this style that is directly responsible for the blues and rock that we hear today.

Robert Johnson was probably the most influential blues guitarist to come out of the Mississippi Delta. Sam Charters, looking for clues to the mysterious life of Johnson, wandered through the Delta area several years ago. He described it as lacking a "sense of permanence. The shacks are crude pine-board boxes, propped up on concrete blocks—at some point in their poor past covered with brown building paper scored to look like brick. The corners of the paper flap in the wind where they've torn loose." Little wonder Muddy Waters told writer Peter Guralnick "I wanted to get out of Mississippi in the worst way," and told Pete Welding that "I didn't *know* it at the time, but I just did *not* like the way things were down there in Mississippi." Since so many eventually left, this thought must have haunted hundreds of thousands of others—musicians and workers alike.

If leaving Mississippi seemed easy, many people's high hopes for a piece of the American Pie were shattered when they got to the North. There were too many workers and too few jobs. In 1925 there were 120,000 blacks living in Chicago; by 1960 that number had reached half a million, most of whom were crowded in the slums. Although the *Defender* a Chicago paper, wrote "If you can freeze in the North and be free, why sweat to death in the South and be a slave?", the reality of that freedom was questionable. Houses on the South Side were crammed with people; sometimes three or four families lived in a single apartment. Discriminatory policies kept many blacks from living in better neighborhoods even when they could afford it. Mahalia Jackson, the great gospel singer, tried to buy a house in a white neighborhood in Chicago, only to be met with threats, lies, and finally bullets shot through her windows. This atmosphere forced the black community to create its own society within the ghetto, which may account for the staggering number of blues clubs in that town.

The despair of being penniless, depressed, and lonely in Chicago is reflected in some of the blues lyrics of the day:

> *I'm just from the country*
> *Never been in your town before;*
> *Lord, I'm broke and hungry*
> *Ain't got no place to go.*

A deep homesickness could come over these refugees after a few harsh winter months and could make the South start to look good again:

> *Chicago and Detroit, folks*
> *Have you heard the news?*
> *Old Dixieland is jumping:*
> *I've got the Southern blues.*

Some did make it. Those that landed good jobs made more money than they could have dreamed of. However, cash in the pocket was no substitute for the intimate hometown life that they were used to and they idealized the old ways and places. Bluesmen have always reflected the feelings of the community and in Chicago it was no different. Many musicians were just getting by, holding down day jobs and playing at night. Son Seals was one of the players who followed the migration north, but he always missed his home state of Arkansas. As he told Peter Guralnick, "I'd go back there today if I could make it economically. You can go down there right now, go out to them country juke-joints and watch them shoot dice and cuss, fry their fish, and barbecue and stuff. You don't have to worry about being mugged, knocking heads, or something all the time." Sunnyland Slim, the blues pianist, came to Chicago because the move offered the opportunity to make records: "I could make good money down in the roadhouses," he told Sam Charters, "but I wanted to be on a record. I don't say I like Chicago, it's dirty and cold and it's got all those politics, but I just come up to Chicago anyway."

Despite the many record companies and clubs that sprouted like mushrooms throughout the South Side, most musicians had to work full-time jobs when they first arrived. A guitarist playing weeknights at a local bar could make five to seven dollars for an evening's work; on weekends he could take home twenty-five dollars for five sets. Muddy Waters worked as a truck driver during the day and played at rent parties and bars at night. Otis Rush worked in the stockyards, and even held a job with the Campbell Soup Company, before playing his first gigs in 1955. Albert King was a bulldozer operator for many years, and claimed proudly that he could "doze a carpet without scratching the floor." He said of his long-sought national recognition: "It's about time I began collecting on some of those dues." B.B. King worked as a disc jockey. Elmore James was a D.J., managed a country club, and held other "straight" jobs when he was not touring. Jimmy Reed was an iron worker in Gary, Indiana. It was only after cutting many records on many different labels that any of these men could settle into a full-time music career.

MISSISSIPPI DELTA ROOTS

Almost all of the musicians we will be discussing and analyzing in this book were originally born and bred in Mississippi before moving on to Chicago. Muddy Waters (McKinley Morganfield) grew up in Clarksdale, Mississippi. Bo Diddley (Elias McDaniel) was born in 1928 in McComb, Mississippi. After arriving in Chicago, Bo Diddley "walked the streets for twelve years before I got someone to listen to me." Otis Rush grew up in Philadelphia, Mississippi, and moved to Chicago in 1949 at the age of fifteen. Howlin' Wolf (Chester Arthur Burnett) came from a little town called West Point, Mississippi, not far from Tupelo. He worked on the Ruleville Plantation, according to writer Arnold Shaw, "driving tractors, fixing fences, picking cotton and pulling corn." After forty years as a part-time musician and full-time farmer, he moved to Chicago. Albert King was the son of a country preacher and grew up in Indianola, Mississippi. The list of Mississippi-born musicians continues and includes Hound Dog Taylor, Johnny Shines, B.B. King, and Elmore James. In order to understand Chicago blues it is imperative to first understand the acoustic country blues that preceded it.

Although many of the country blues guitarists spent time in Chicago, their most creative and inventive days were spent wandering around the small towns of the Delta region. Robert Johnson, Charley Patton, Skip James, Bukka White, and many more perfected their craft in their home states of Texas, Arkansas, and Mississippi. They would play at fish-fries and parties, or on dusty town streets to make a few dollars and then move on. In their travels they often crossed paths; perhaps traveling a while together, exchanging musical ideas and good wishes before parting. Robert Johnson certainly was a compulsive wanderer and no one knew when he would show up or when he would leave. Johnny Shines told Sam Charters about Johnson's traveling habits: "He would just pick up and walk off and leave you standing there playing. And you wouldn't see Robert no more maybe in two or three weeks. . . . He was a kind of peculiar fellow."

All of these players were self-taught and did not have the benefit of books, videotapes, or teachers to give them formal lessons. They experimented on the most primitive instruments. Albert King described his first guitar as "A little cigar-box for the body and a little tree I cut off and shaved up to make a neck." It took a keen eye, a certain aggressiveness, and great determination for a young guitarist to learn in those days.

One of the surest instruction methods was to corner musicians who passed through town. Styles can be traced from one player to the next. Robert Johnson bugged Son House to teach him, who described Johnson as a "little boy standing around" who would wait until his mother went to bed "and then he'd get out the window to make it" to the dangerously rough Saturday night dances. When Son House or Charley Patton set their guitars down, Robert would sneak away and practice on one of them "running people crazy with it."

Obsessed with this six-stringed instrument, Robert Johnson left his work in the fields and ran away from home. The next time Son House saw him, "he was so good. . .when he finished all our mouths were standing open." Although he was vastly admired by his contemporaries, no one at the time could have realized what a profound effect Robert Johnson would have on blues players over the next thirty years. His disciples include Muddy Waters, Johnny Shines, and Elmore James (in his obvious quotations of Johnson's bass-string boogie lines and whining slide riffs), as well as rock players like Jimi Hendrix, Eric Clapton, and Johnny Winter.

With a guitar slung over his shoulder, Johnson traveled all over Mississippi, Arkansas, and Missouri before working his way north for a brief stay in Chicago. Johnny Shines remembered him playing for a small audience in St. Louis. He told Sam Charters: "He was playing slow and passionate, and when he had quit, I noticed no one was saying anything. Then I realized they were crying—both men and women."

His infectious guitar style took ideas from country blues and expanded them. He played fingerstyle in the open-E tuning usually used by bottleneck players. He kept a rock-steady bass line with his thumb. His fingers picked the melody in the higher strings, but with sudden stops, bends, and brilliant rhythmic twists thrown in.

Robert Johnson's life, despite exhaustive research by Sam Charters and other blues scholars, is sketchy at best. We do know that he was a high-roller with many women admirers. When he was poisoned (or stabbed) by a betrayed girlfriend (or jealous husband) in 1938, he was approximately twenty-six. Most of the lyrics to his songs deal with his rather bleak vision of the world, and perhaps he knew how it would end when he sang "Hello Satan, I believe it's time to go." His death quietly brought an era of country blues to a close, until the music of Johnson and many of his contemporaries was pulled into the limelight during the blues revival of the sixties.

If Robert Johnson had a profound effect on Muddy Waters and Elmore James, Charley Patton had no less influence on Howlin' Wolf. Charley "started me out playing," Wolf told Pete Welding. "We got through picking cotton at night, we'd go hang out with him...he used to play out at the plantation, at different homes...there were no clubs like nowadays."

Patton was born in the 1880s in Mississippi and, although his name is all but forgotten, his influence is still felt a hundred years later. Patton's style is described as offbeat by Wolf who said that it took a very good musician to try to follow him. In fact Patton wasn't the only country bluesman who, used to playing solo, would make chord changes when he wanted to rather than stick to the twelve- or sixteen-bar form so common today.

His style so influenced Howlin' Wolf that his musical interests grew to encompass more than his neighbors' "old-fashioned folk singing." He began to listen to what was considered modern for his time: the Mississippi Sheiks, Lonnie Johnson, Tampa Red, and Blind Blake. While the influence of white country-music on black blues is not often discussed (one usually hears about the effect of blues on country music), Wolf acknowledges his fascination with Jimmie Rodgers, and recalls his attempts at imitating aspects of the Singing Brakeman's style. He freely admits that, despite his musical respect for Rodgers, his own attempts at yodeling sounded more like "growlin' and howlin'."

GOING ELECTRIC

Muddy Waters, talking about his early, legendary bands said, "We were doing the stuff like we did years ago down in Mississippi." But there was a difference. Electric guitars had replaced acoustics with their loud, raspy, and sustained tones. "You can't hear an acoustic in a bar," Muddy said. The use of electric guitars was to change the nature of the blues. Generally, the guitar in a combo was a rhythm instrument. Even the loud F-holed guitars could not be heard above a piano, bass, or drums. Electrification allowed guitars to cut through the other sounds and the guitar took its place beside the sax, harp, and piano as a lead instrument. After a while, it was the guitarists who began to steal the show as hot lead-players began to front their own bands.

Electric guitars took lighter strings than acoustics and could be played easier and faster. Blues players found that they could bend and sustain treble strings better (T-Bone Walker was probably the first to use an unwound G-string) and an entire technique was based on the "new" vibrato. String bending was the technique that led blues guitarists down a different stylistic path from the jazz players of the time.

Within the blues community, each player approached the music in his own unique way. Even among the three Kings—Freddie, Albert, and B.B.—there is a vast difference in tone, style, and point of view. Freddie plays a cutting, hard-edged, almost choppy style which is evident in his earlier work (see "Hide Away" or "San-Ho-Zay"); Albert is sly and sensual with his string-bending; B.B is completely at ease with his vibrato and will dart through phrases, stopping suddenly to bend a string and create a tension that resolves as his solo develops. Albert King picks with is bare thumb, while Freddie King uses a thumbpick and fingerpicks for his solos. B.B. uses the traditional plastic flatpick. Albert is one of several guitar players (including Jimi Hendrix) to play left-handed, with the guitar upside down and backward. Freddie King, like Albert and B.B., does not play any slide guitar. He confided to Dan Forte that "my fingers are too heavy; I play too hard. I do some of the same licks though, as Elmore James, Earl Hooker, and guys like that."

Of all the blues guitarists we will be studying, B.B. King can probably claim the most sophisticated influences. He was an ardent fan of old-timers Bukka White and Blind Lemon Jefferson, was "*crazy* about Charlie Christian," and loved listening to Django Reinhardt. Arnold Shaw, in *Honkers and Shouters*, makes some interesting points about B.B.'s integration of these styles with the blues: "Ninth chords are a staple of B.B.'s style, instead of minor (blues) notes played against major chords (I IV V), as in Delta or country blues. King uses single-string runs and jazz-blues riffs, making the instrument less percussive and more melodic." B.B. himself credits T-Bone Walker for this jazzy sound: "He was the first guy I ever heard play blues with a ninth chord." T-Bone Walker is best known for his masterful blues hit "Stormy Monday," but he was a highly influential guitar wizard. By playing a Gibson *ES 335* through a Fender amp, using an unwound G-string to facilitate bends, and as B.B. described, "a measured touch," T-Bone was a master of tone.

Clearly, choice of instruments somewhat depended on the particular style of the artists. Bo Diddley first played his famous "hand-jive" rhythm-riff on a large, hollow-bodied Gretsch guitar; a versatile instrument that could produce not only a clean rhythm sound but a biting, high-pitched lead. Blues players were split between hollow- and solid-body guitars, and there is evidence that solid-bodies such as Gibson *ES* models and Fender *Strats* and *Telecasters* were also very popular.

A WORD ON GUITARS

Nothing is more important to a guitarist than his guitar. The instrument was made to be cuddled, caressed, and loved. Players sometimes call their instruments by a woman's name (like B.B. King's Lucille) often to the dismay of their own neglected girlfriends. I don't know of any woman guitarists who have named their instruments, but a glance at Libba Cotten fingerpicking her Martin flattop, or Bonnie Raitt playing slide on her Strat, shows a profound love for their instruments. When a guitar is stolen, smashed to splinters on an airplane, or lost, no amount of insurance money can ever console the heartbroken owner.

In the old days, blues singers clung to their guitars as if they were liferafts on a stormy ocean. The rough-and-tumble bars where they worked to pay the rent must have caused ulcers in more than one nervous musician. Late at night, punches and bottles would get thrown, and fights often ended in someone's serious injury or murder. Johnny Shines recently recalled these fights to a reporter in Providence, Rhode Island with the fondness of a veteran who had survived the battles of a past war: "When they had fights you'd cover your guitar and hope that if anybody threw a bottle it hit *you* instead of the guitar."

Although Chicago blues is generally played on electric guitar, most players continue to keep up their acoustic technique. Some of the older songs were meant to be played on flat-tops, and sound better that way. The first electric guitars—played by pioneers like Charlie Christian, T-Bone Walker, and Les Paul—were hollow-body instruments with magnetic pickups mounted in them. These instruments produced the mellow tone that we associate with swing and bebop. In the late forties and early fifties, guitar manufacturers—most notably Fender and Gibson—started experimenting with new pickups mounted in wooden solid-body and semi-hollow-body guitars. The results were staggering. The new Fender *Stratocasters, Telecasters,* and Gibson *Les Pauls* quickly invaded the growing blues and rock guitar market. These new solid-body guitars were loud, brash, and versatile without feeding back like hollow-bodies. Improvements made in pickups, tone control, neck action, and string gauge begun during those years have set the standard against which all electric guitars are judged to this day. There is nothing that compares with the sexy, gutsy, wailing, funky, rasping, and irresistible sounds made by those guitars of the fifties.

ON CHOOSING A GUITAR

Walking into any guitar store in a major city will reveal a selection of vintage Gibson, Guild, Fender, and Gretsch guitars for sale at wildly inflated prices. If you can afford one you might as well go ahead and indulge—they are the best instruments for playing blues. If you haven't got a trust fund, a hit record, or a lucky lottery ticket, you don't have to stand there gaping: A great guitar does not a great guitarist make. There are plenty of excellent guitars on the market that will suit your needs and allow you to pay the rent.

Blues players are split in their choice of solid-body or semi-hollow-body guitars. B.B. King currently plays a semi-hollow-body Gibson *ES 355 SVW* which produces a wide variety of tones. (Of course, Gibson did build the guitar just for him.) Albert King fancies a solid-body Gibson *Flying V* for its biting treble tones while Buddy Guy tends to prefer Fender *Stratocasters*. You will have to decide for yourself which type of guitar best suits your needs. It's always good to bring a friend or a professional along with you when you are looking to buy. Because the guitar market is so huge, and the decision process so personal, we can only give you general advice as to what to look for and what to avoid when buying an instrument:

> Make sure that the guitar is comfortable when you hold it. This may seem obvious, but a guitar that's too big will directly affect the way you play, and could even cause back problems.
>
> The action should be light, and the strings shouldn't buzz: You should be able to fret chords up the neck without strain, producing clear tones each time. If you notice any small defects with the action, keep in mind that most good guitars have adjustable bridges and necks. A good repairman can help you set up a guitar to meet your needs.
>
> A guitar with a truss rod in the neck will prevent pressure from the strings from warping the neck.
>
> See if the instrument is covered by a guarantee from the manufacturer. This makes it the manufacturer's responsibility to correct any inherent defects and protects you from getting stuck with a lemon.

Most good guitars, particularly acoustics, improve with age. They mature according to the quality of the wood with which they were constructed. As the guitar is played over the years, the wood becomes more resonant until finally the instrument sings with a rich and particularly unique personal tone. Instruments branded as "vintage" are not merely older and better instruments: They are often priced according to their value as collectables. While certain prestige instruments may have the sound that you are looking for, you might do better by listening to a guitar rather than a salesman interested in selling you an art object. Our personal choice for a combination of a great funky sound with economic value is an old Fender *Jaguar*. If you can find one at a reasonable price snatch it up.

If you are considering a used instument:

> Always compare prices when it is possible.
>
> Try to verify the age of the instrument by running a check on the serial number with the manufacturer.

Check for parts that may have been replaced, thus lowering the value of the instrument: Are the neck, bridge, and pickups original or new? Original parts will insure the resale value of your instrument.

BASIC TABLATURE AND HOW TO USE IT

The music in this book has been written in both standard notation and guitar tablature. Tablature is useful even to those who can read music because it is a graphic representation of the guitar.

Tablature is written with six horizontal lines, each one representing one of the six strings. The treble strings are on top, and the bass is on the bottom.

A number written on a line shows what fret is to be played. For example, a C note played on the A string would be written like this:

A C chord would appear like this:

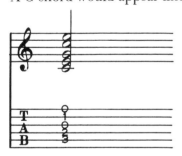

An arched line with an *h* over it indicates a hammer-on.

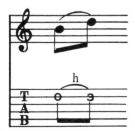

An arched line with a *p* over it indicates a pulloff.

A slide from one note to another is indicated like this:

A slide up to a specific note from an arbitrary point on the neck is shown with a straight diagonal line slanted like this:

A slide down to a specific note from any point on the neck is notated with a line slanted in the opposite direction.

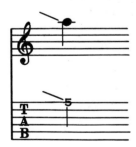

RHYTHM NOTATION

Strumming patterns have been notated with slash marks. One slash mark is equivalent to a quarter note. The following example indicates four strums per measure with each chord changing on the first beat.

An accent mark (>) is used when a particular beat should be stressed.

Individual time values are notated as follows.

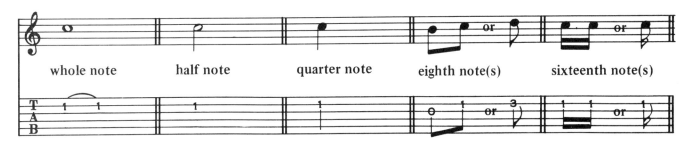

Maxwell Street, Chicago

BENDS, VIBRATO, AND TREMOLO

> I could never use a bottleneck...so I learned to trill my finger. That's how I get the vibrato.
> B.B. King in a conversation with Arnold Shaw

> I always concentrated on my singing guitar sound —more of a sustained note...the bending note sound...the string-squeezing sound.
> Albert King in an interview with Dan Forte

> He used a plain (unwound) G because you couldn't quiver or bend a G. Bone said bending the note made the sound richer, it put more feeling into it —a little more soul.
> Lowell Fulson discussing T-Bone Walker with Kevin and Peter Sheridan

In a funny way slide guitar was partially responsible for the string bending that we associate with B.B. King and Albert King. B.B. King, in an interview with Arnold Shaw, put it this way: "When I first settled in Memphis, around 1946, I did stay with Bukka White for about a year. He played with a slide most of the time, and I just loved the sound of that. I could never use a bottleneck on my fingers as he did, so I learned to trill my finger. That's how I get the vibrato." Albert King, on the other hand, claims he "couldn't make the runs" so he took to bending strings.

In blues, the most often used bends are done on the third and second strings, although all strings have been bent by players at one time or another. The only way to really get this technique right is to listen to the best benders live or on record: Albert, B.B., or Freddie King, as well as Buddy Guy, Otis Rush, or T-Bone Walker.

We have notated bends by using an arched line with a *b* over it. In this example, the second string at the seventh fret is bent up a whole step—from an F♯ to a G♯. The number or note in parentheses, indicates the pitch that you'll be bending up to. Your left hand doesn't actually move to the ninth fret, but stays on the seventh and bends the string until a G♯ is sounded. The first note is always played quickly, and the second is held the full time-value.

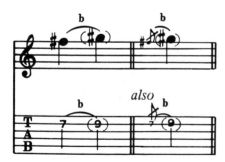

16

An *r* signals the release of a bend.

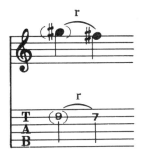

Generally, the highest two strings (E and B) should be *pushed* (bent by *pushing* toward you) and the lower strings *pulled* away from you.

Note: Repeated bending can often throw your strings out of tune, so be aware of possible intonation problems.

There are two kinds of vibrato possible on guitar. Both are commonly used by most blues guitarists. The subtler variety is achieved by keeping the fingertip planted on the string and moving the hand back and forth in line with the neck. The fingertip does not actually move but sort of rolls with the movement of the hand. This type of vibrato is similar to that used by classical guitarists and violinists and does not produce a change in pitch but rather in intensity. With the sustain possible on an electric guitar this technique can produce a variety of effects depending on the amount of energy you put into it and the speed at which you do it.

The other kind of vibrato is simply a series of quick bends and releases. This vibrato is especially effective on notes that have already been bent up but in most cases should be kept fairly unexaggerated. In other words; unless you are going for a wild, uncontrolled sound; keep the pitch variation to less than a half step.

Since the choice of which vibrato to use is largely personal and is further dictated by technical considerations, we have not attempted to distinguish between the two in the notation of the examples and transcriptions. Either type, or a combination of the two, may be used when you see the following symbol.

Tremolo is a fast alternation of two notes. When you see this symbol play only the first note and then rapidly hammer-on or pulloff to the second note. Keep alternating for the duration indicated (in the case of the example below, a half note).

TO PICK OR NOT TO PICK

Albert King plays with his bare thumb, and still manages to keep up a percussive pick-like sound. Freddie King uses a thumbpick as well as a metal fingerpick on his first finger. By alternating his thumb and fingers, he can duplicate the sound of the up- and down-strokes usually done with a flatpick alone. Perhaps it's this right-hand technique that makes Freddie so proficient when playing "Dust My Broom" or any other blues classic on acoustic guitar. Wes Montgomery, the jazz guitarist, played with his thumb, and would take incredible solos in octaves at breakneck speed. He developed his "impossible" technique on his own, and may never have discovered his unique style had he received only formal training. "No one ever told me *not* to do it!" he explained to me several years ago.

The point of this digression is simply to point out that while most electric guitarists prefer to use a flatpick, there are countless alternatives. Anyone who teaches that *his* way is the *only* way is out of touch with the history of colorful and idiosyncratic guitar players. In light of Mr. Montgomery's statement, we won't attempt to give you the last word on technique: If you feel like picking with your knuckles, go ahead and try it. You have nothing to lose but your skin.

If you should decide to give the more conventional flatpick a whirl, try experimenting with all three kinds: thin, medium, and heavy. Each one has a different feel and results in a different tone. If urging you to try each available thickness sounds painfully obvious, I can say that it was only through borrowing a hard pick in an emergency did I discover how well it worked for me. It had never occurred to me to try something other than my medium pick before, even though "no one ever told me not to do it."

You will have to use up- *and* down-strokes when playing single-string phrases with a flatpick. If you are a beginner, you may find the pick to be somewhat cumbersome and the motion of alternating up and down a bit foreign. Try taking a pick with you wherever you go, practicing on a spiral notebook or your belt buckle. You'll be suprised at how quickly your playing will progress, and your thumb and forefinger will begin to feel lonely when they aren't holding that triangular bit of plastic. Remember to keep your wrist loose and not to grip the pick tightly, but rather rest it on the joint of the first finger using your thumb to give it the slightest resistance.

The following exercise is tedious and tasteless, but will yield great results in strengthening both your right and left hands. It is the manual equivalent of a tongue-twister, and is worth doing even five short minutes a day if it's done every day. Although it's shown in first position on the E string, it should be practiced up the neck and on all six strings.

Well, wasn't that fun! Perhaps you'll feel better if we told you that many first-rate players warm up with this exercise. It stretches the fingers and stimulates the mind. You'll never outgrow it, no matter how many fancy riffs you can play with your eyes closed.

STRUMMING

Strumming an electric guitar is actually a difficult task that takes great control. Your *touch* must be developed, and an awareness of the sounds that you are producing must become an integral part of your study. By touch, we mean your personal approach to the guitar. You should always have high standards: Is your playing clean? Do your strings buzz? Do you fret and strum each note so that they ring evenly? Are only the right strings ringing? Are you playing with ease? Is your tempo steady? These are basic standards that should always be met no matter what your level.

When strumming rhythm parts, try to make sure that the strings do not sound "out of control." The natural sustain on an electric guitar makes this a common problem. You can prevent this by *damping*, a technique that mutes the strings as you're playing. This is a tricky, subtle technique that is almost impossible to describe without actually showing it in person. The basic idea behind it is that your left or right hand, properly placed, can control the tone and the length of a chord. Keep the following ways of approaching this in mind, and feel free to experiment as you continue with the exercises in this book.

There are three ways to damp the strings of a guitar. The first is to lift your left-hand fingers from the fretboard after strumming a chord, but continue to touch the strings lightly—just enough to muffle the sound. The second way is to lightly touch the strings with the fleshy part of your left hand while strumming. Finally, you can damp the strings with your right hand by using your palm up near the bridge. All of these techniques will mute the chord and prevent continuous ringing.

Right-hand damping

If there is one thing that we have learned from studying Chicago blues guitarists, it's that true value is not in what you play, or how much you play, but how you play it. Of course good technique is essential, but it is only a means of self-expression. Some people prefer to take a simple approach to music, and can squeeze emotion out of a single note. Others can achieve a simple but strong emotion with fancy chords and riffs. Both approaches are equally valid: We believe that music is not a contest, but is only worth playing or listening to if some message gets conveyed through it. As you study, you may find certain musical ideas beyond your understanding and ability. Make an effort to grasp them but if they continue to elude you, let them. Part of growing and learning is accepting what you cannot do, and in taking pride in your own particular achievements. B.B. King admires the unique improvisations of Django Reinhardt, but makes no attempt to master that style—he takes from it what he needs. Similarly, we hope that you will take what you need from this book.

TWELVE-BAR BLUES

> You'll always be able to hear twelve-bar blues. Always. It's the backbone of American music. Everything else comes from that.
> Rufus Thomas

> He had no conception of a twelve-bar blues. It could be eight-and-a-half, thirteen-and-a-quarter or what have you. The musicians would be all over the place. But he had a wonderful feeling...
> Bobby Shad discussing (with Arnold Shaw) a recording session with Lightnin' Hopkins.

Twelve-bar blues, as Rufus Thomas points out, is the common meeting ground for all musicians, whether they play blues, pop, rock, or jazz. When players meet to jam for the first time, they inevitably choose a blues to warm up with—they all know the changes and everyone can solo. We have given several examples of twelve-bar blues below. Remember: You must be able to play these changes in every key, so get ready to transpose to B♭, A♭, and other keys with ominous sounding names.

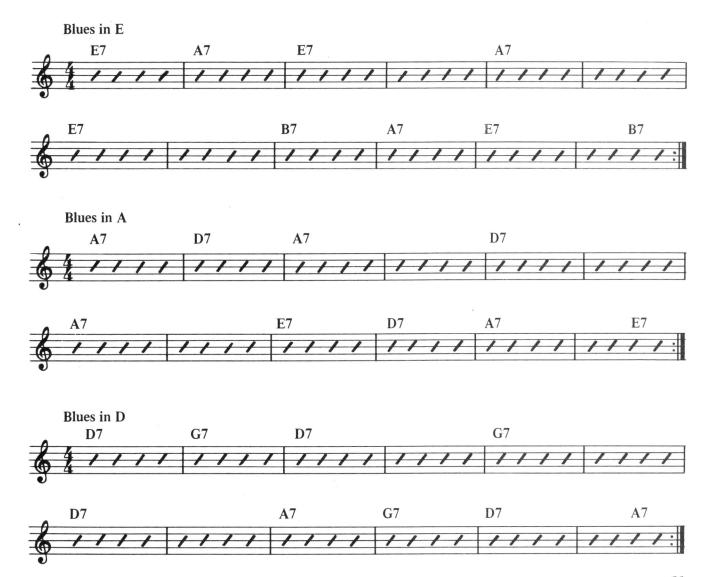

Before trying the next two twelve-bar blues progressions in A♭ and E♭, go over the chord forms given below.

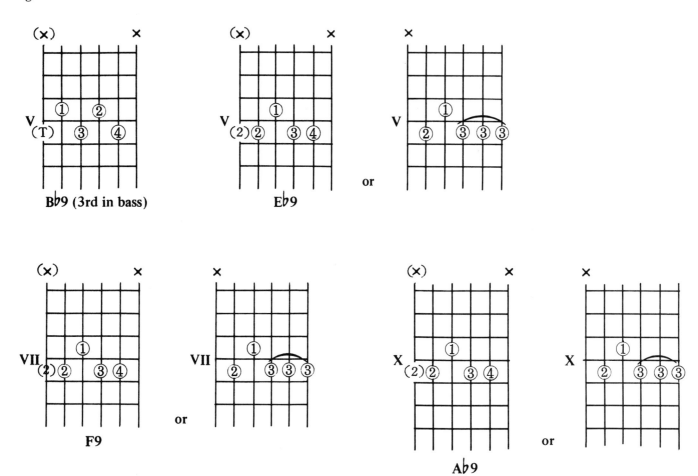

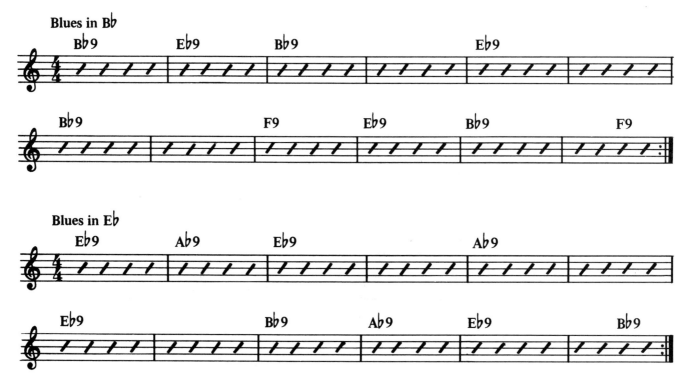

THE BLUES TURNAROUND

A turnaround is a series of notes, or chord changes that occurs in the last two measures of a blues progression and signals the repeat of the entire twelve bars. Over the years many turnarounds have become cliches, but there are still a few among them that are classic, and seem more familiar—like an old friend—than boring.

The turnaround given below is directly from the country blues. It is for the key of E, and should be followed by a B7 chord, before swinging back into the top of the blues. This turnaround, and many like it, was played extensively in the 1920s and 30s. You can hear it on old recordings including those of Robert Johnson, Muddy Waters, and Son House.

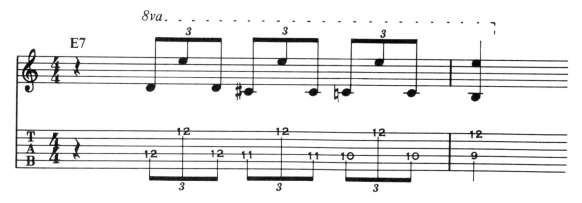

This next example is a more sophisticated variation of the basic turnaround shown above. Notice the counter-movement: The melodic line on the second string descends while the fourth string has an ascending harmony.

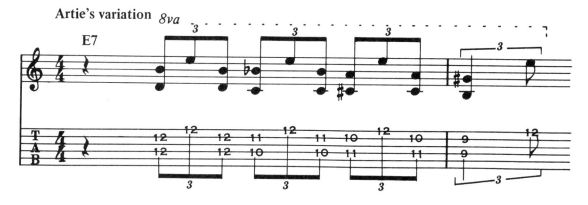

Turnarounds can get a little more complicated. Here's one that uses only chords, but is set in a jazz-style twelve-bar blues. Use the diagrams to help with the chords that you don't already know.

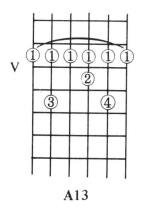

A13

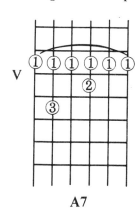

A7

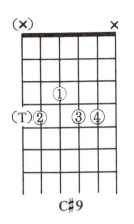 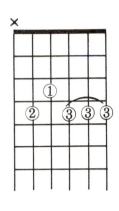 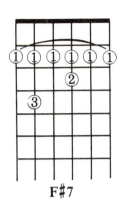

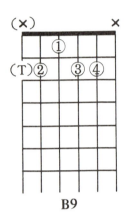 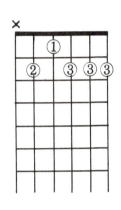

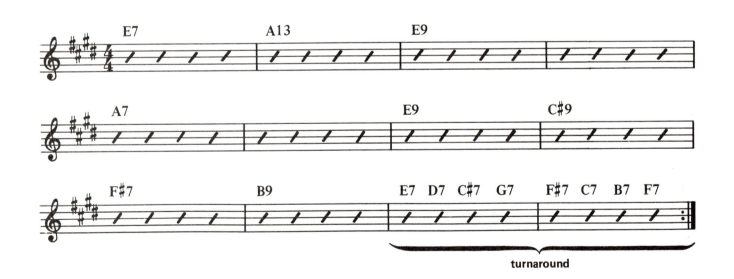

Chords for turnaround

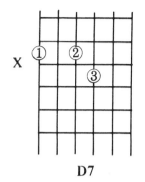 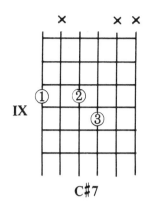 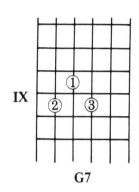 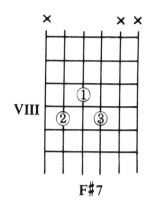

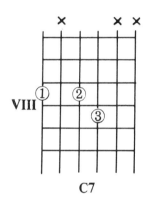 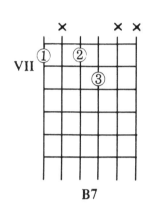 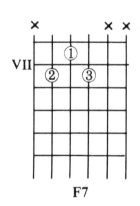 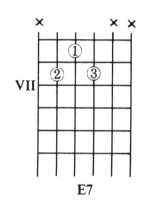

THE SHUFFLE LICK

'Cause I'm gonna play the high-class joints
I'm gonna play the low-class joints;
And baby, I'm gonna play the honky-tonks.
"Honky Tonk" by Bobby "Blue" Bland

Although today we can hear Chicago blues in concert halls, it started out as dance music. The shuffle can be a way of moving on a dance floor or the beat that makes you want to do it. Shuffle rhythm is the backbone of most Chicago blues, and Jimmy Reed comes immediately to mind as the man who cultivated its country blues roots in city soil.

When Reed came North he got work at a steel mill in Gary, Indiana. His lunch hours were spent playing and singing, so that by the time he began recording for Vee-Jay Records in the mid fifties he felt that he'd paid his dues. He finally received national recognition around 1960 when "Big Boss Man" and "Bright Lights, Big City" (one of the first country-western/blues crossover hits) hit the charts.

Every song that he played, from his popular hits "You Don't Have to Go," "Big Boss Man," and the classic "Ain't That Lovin' You Baby," to his lesser known songs, all relied on the shuffle lick.

The shuffle lick is also used extensively by Chuck Berry, Elmore James, Muddy Waters, and other players who rely on a boogie bass. In fact, it goes as far back as Robert Johnson, who used it to accompany his singing and when he played slide. He would skillfully polish off a melodic riff up the neck, and jump back to the bass notes to continue the shuffle.

Whether the early blues piano players, like Jimmy Yancee, Pine Top Smith, and Meade Lux Lewis, were taking their ideas from guitar players, or vice versa, can't really be decided accurately. But even sophisticated boogie bass-lines, played by musicians like Otis Spann, work well on acoustic or electric guitar.

Not only did guitarists find that they could duplicate these bass lines, but they found that they could play the melody or a solo as well. There were many approaches taken to this tricky finger-picking style, but a steady thumb was essential to them all. This example is from Lightnin' Hopkins, who always keeps a steady $\frac{4}{4}$ or $\frac{2}{4}$ beat going on his fifth or sixth string.

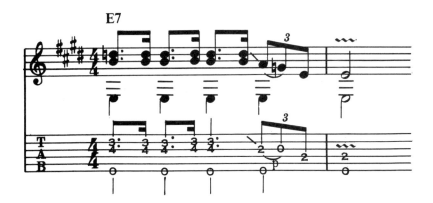

The shuffle lick that's used as a basic structure in contemporary blues, R&B, and rock and roll, has several variations. Although the easiest positions are found in the keys of A, E, D, and G, you should be able to play a twelve-bar blues based on the shuffle lick in *all* keys. You will have to bar across the neck when playing in keys like B♭ or E♭.

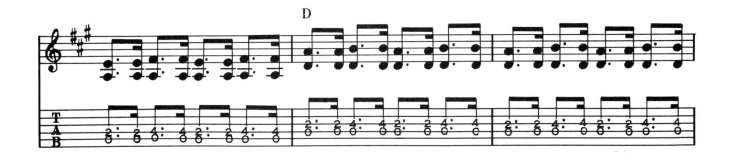

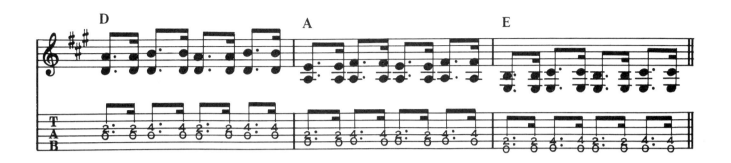
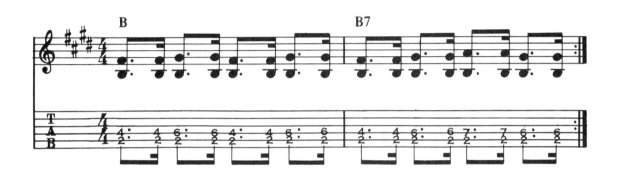
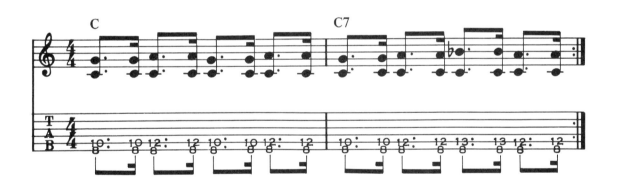

Here's an example of the Memphis version of the shuffle lick in the key of A. You might try hammering-on that second sixteenth note in the fourth beat.

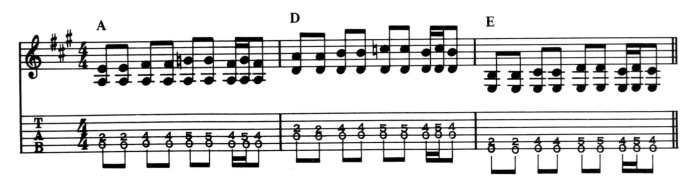

BLUES SCALES

Almost all blues melodies, solos, and riffs are based on the notes found in the *pentatonic* blues scale. Once you've learned the scale in several keys, you will have a solid musical vocabulary that you can use again and again.

Pentatonic scales, unlike major scales, consist of only five notes. The third and seventh degrees are flatted, thus making licks and solos based on the pentatonic blues scale work remarkably well with seventh and minor-seventh chords. Blues have always straddled the fence between major and minor, and it is the musical paradox of minor solos played against major chords that gives the blues an excitement all its own.

The scales shown below are all given in the key of A. Except for the first one, they are written in closed positions and can be played in any key. For example, by moving the exercise up one fret you can play the scale in B♭; move it up one more fret and you will be in B, and so on. If you are only using tablature to learn these scales, check with the fingering used in the music to get the correct left-hand patterns.

Pentatonic blues scale I (open position)

Pentatonic blues scale II (closed position)

Pentatonic blues scale III (closed position)

31

Pentatonic blues scale IV (closed position; two octaves)

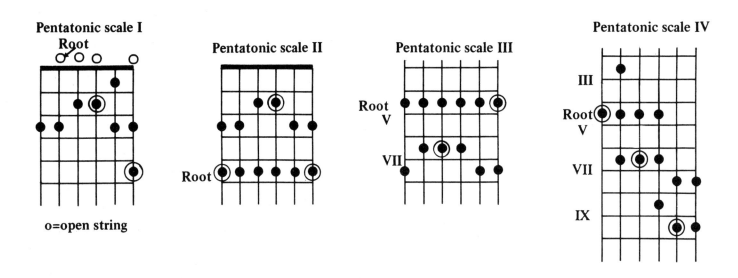

Pentatonic scale I
o=open string

Pentatonic scale II

Pentatonic scale III

Pentatonic scale IV

Blues scales alone can sound stiff and cold which is not what the blues is all about. Below, we've given you a sampling of some essential, expressive riffs from the playing of B.B. King, Albert King, and others, so you can see how the scales can be used.

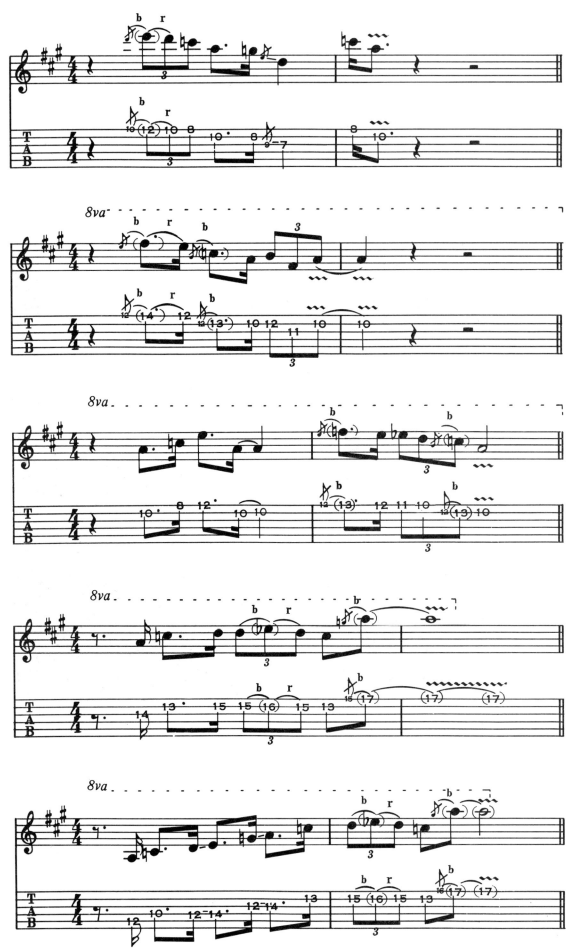

Bo, Marva Waters, Muddy Waters, Marie Dixon, and Pops Taylor

BOTTLENECK AND SLIDE GUITAR

> Sonny House...He used to have a neck of a bottle over his finger, little finger, touching the strings to make them sing. That's where I got the idea from. You break it off, hold it under a flame until it melts and gets smooth.
>
> Muddy Waters

One day, perhaps around the turn of the century, in a small hot Louisiana or Mississippi town, some adventurous guitarist happened to move a piece of glass across the neck of his (or her) guitar. It made a whiny, slithering sound on the strings, a moody tone not unlike the emotional wail of a Southern blues singer. In fact, the sound was so compatible with the blues, the guitarist filed down the broken end of a bottle so that it fit snugly on his third finger, and developed a vibrant new style of playing: *Bottleneck*. We will probably never know who was the first to play bottleneck guitar— perhaps the idea came to several guitarists around the same time, an idea whose time had come. We do know that many of the early blues artists to appear on record, like Son House, Bukka White, and Robert Johnson, had all mastered the style by the 1920s. Bottleneck, or *slide* guitar as it later became called, was to have an immense effect on blues guitarists from Muddy Waters to Elmore James to Hound Dog Taylor. Eventually, most blues players began using a sawed-off piece of metal tubing instead of glass. Despite slight variations in tone caused by the difference in materials, the slide effects remained the same. Initially developed on acoustic guitar, the slide style was perfectly suited to the raw, electric blues that swept Chicago in the late 1940s.

If we were to pick one slide riff that says "Chicago" when it is played on guitar, it would have to be the sly, gutsy phrase that Elmore James made famous with his version of "Dust My Broom." Tune your third, fourth, and fifth strings up to get into open-E tuning (low-to-high: E B E G♯ B E) and try the basic riff.

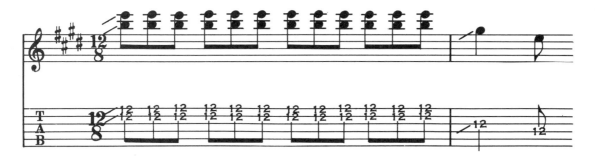

Robert Johnson first recorded this classic in 1936, playing the riff fingerstyle against a steady shuffle bass-line. And although Elmore James had a somewhat successful hit record with the tune in 1953, it can be traced clearly back to its country-blues origins. Homesick James, Elmore's older cousin, claims to have learned the riff from an old-time (anonymous) bluesman in Florida, who played "with a guitar layin' in his lap, using a jackknife for a slide." The riff can also be found on early bottleneck recordings of Son House, Bukka White, and others—particularly Robert Johnson.

Elmore James began playing bottleneck on a very crude guitar when he was just twelve years old and living in Mississippi. A natural on guitar, he quickly began playing at local parties and fish-fries, jamming the blues with legendary artists like Arthur "Big Boy" Crudup ("Rock Me, Baby") and Johnny Temple. It was only a matter of time before Elmore James crossed musical paths with

Robert Johnson, who had a profound effect on him. Robert Johnson taught James the version of "Dust" that was to become famous in Chicago many years later. The riff is a 'hook' tailor-made for shuffle style Chicago blues, with just enough space between phrases to allow the rhythm to emerge.

Since this riff is played in fast triplets, your right hand must be agile enough to keep the tempo. Try alternating up- and down-strokes on the second and first strings. If you choose a slow tempo, we recommend consecutive up-strokes.

From a technical standpoint, slide guitar is somewhat tricky. Many guitarists use the third finger of the left hand for the slide, though the pinky may be used to leave the other fingers free for fretting. Very often a riff will be played with the slide, followed by standard chords or rhythm parts played with the fingers. You may, therefore, have trouble controlling the slide at first. It will feel awkward and bulky and may click against the frets or the side of your guitar. There are a couple of tricks you might consider to speed up your progress with the slide. First, like an oversized ring, the slide must fit your finger. It should be tight enough to stay on without stopping your circulation. I'm embarrassed to admit that I once got a piece of metal tubing stuck on my third finger. The harder I tried to yank it off, the more my finger swelled.

"Very stylish," my doctor quipped, threatening to have my brains examined. "Do you stick your fingers in metal tubes often?" I debated leaving the slide on my finger for good as a testament to my dedication as a blues guitarist, but when the doctor had shrunk my finger with numbing ice-packs, I felt a surge of relief.

I considered, for a while, playing Hawaiian style, holding the guitar on my lap with the slide between my thumb and second finger. This is a good way to see the frets and control pressure while playing—particularly in open-D or E tuning. As you can see in this chord chart, the I, IV, and V chords can be found by simply fretting the twelfth, fifth, and seventh frets with the slide.

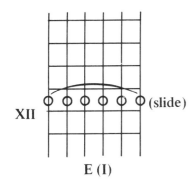
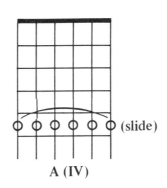
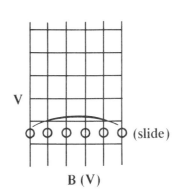

As you can hear, all of the strings can be fretted when the guitar is tuned to an open chord. By playing with the guitar on your lap, you should be able to learn your way around quickly. And it is a quite legitimate technique used on the *Dobro* (an instrument used basically in country-and-western music) and on the metal-bodied *National* guitar, a favorite with bluesmen. Many Dobros and Nationals are set up with a raised bridge that keeps the strings high above the fingerboard. A metal resonator gives these instruments a whiny, almost electric sound, especially when the body itself is made of metal. Metal slides and metal fingerpicks assured a loudness favored by streetsingers who had to compete with city noise. Eventually, electric instruments were developed, including the 'lap steel', Hawaiian guitar, and eventually, the complex 'pedal steel' guitar. So when you practice in this manner, you will be following a long established approach to the slide. Still, the vast majority of Chicago blues guitarists played slide guitar by holding the guitar in normal position.

One of the problems in slide playing is finding notes in blues riffs, since accuracy and speed are often a problem. Try playing the high E and B notes, the first two strings on the twelfth fret, and then slide them down to the tenth fret.

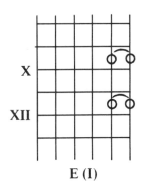

E (I)

If you find that the strings are ringing *behind* the fret where the slide rests, you must damp them by lightly dragging the fleshy part of your left-hand index finger. You may also want to damp strings near the bridge with your right hand. Not only is this essential to clean playing, it will also become part of your funky, slightly muted rhythm playing for other blues ideas.

Once you find the notes in these exercises, you will want to try sliding into them; that is, start a fret or two below the note you want and run the slide up to it. At times, you may want to slide several frets for dramatic effect. Here are some slide riffs to try. (These are all in open-E tuning.)

38

When you arrive at a note you want to hold, vibrato is an essential part of your technique. This can best be done by quickly moving your slide back and forth over the note. This is more easily understood by *hearing* it done and we recommend you listen closely to any Muddy Waters, Homesick James, or Elmore James recording.

Open-E tuning also has some blues-related chords that can easily be fretted.

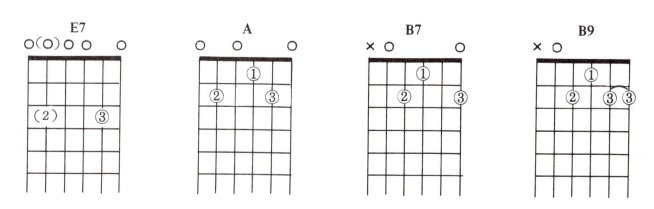

Most slide players will grab chords with their first and second fingers between slide riffs. This is tricky to do, but essential when playing in standard tuning. Here is a twelve-bar solo in standard tuning that will show you what we mean.

A good slide player should be able to fret rhythm chords with his fingers and then break into lead riffs with the slide. Of course, all of the notes of the normal blues scales are available to a slide player, and we would suggest practicing the blues scales we have outlined earlier with the slide.

An important consideration when playing slide guitar: 'Intonation' (playing in tune) is essential to slide players since they have to rely on their ears to know when to stop a slide. Many players have a tendency to overshoot the fret desired and play the note sharp. Slide guitar out of tune can sound nasty. Pay attention to the sound!

To finish out this brief slide survey we would like to give you a Hound Dog Taylor solo to work on.

Hound Dog Taylor is a regular performer in Chicago's South Side and although he's not well-known outside of his native city, he has a magnetic attraction to other bluesmen there. He was born in 1915 in Natchez, Mississippi, and learned to play guitar when he was in his early twenties. Hound Dog, a good friend of Elmore James, is a master of funky electric slide guitar and plays mostly in open-E tuning. We have transcribed his James-inspired solo to "Wild about You" which can be heard with all its roughhewn power on Alligator 4701.

Wild about You

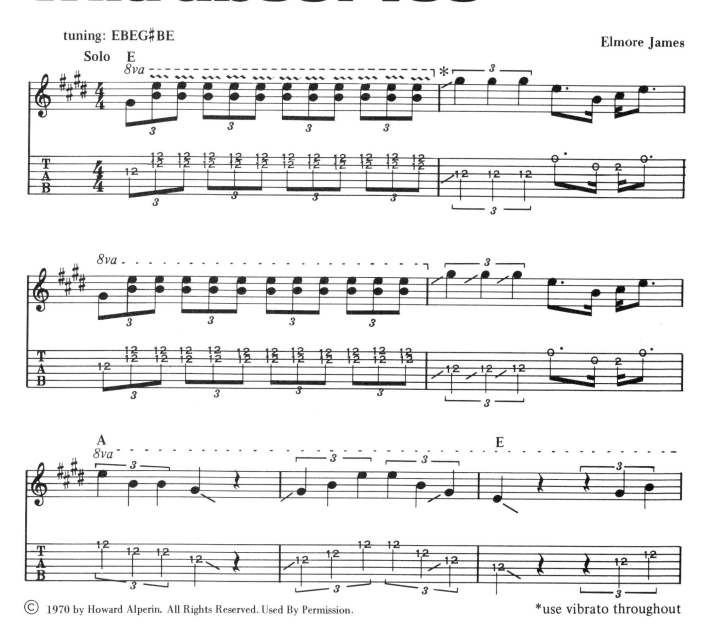

tuning: EBEG#BE

Elmore James

© 1970 by Howard Alperin. All Rights Reserved. Used By Permission.

*use vibrato throughout

Rhythm accompaniment for "Wild about You" (open tuning)

tuning: EBEG#BE

Rhythm accompaniment for "Wild about You." (standard tuning)

RIFFS

> Instrumental jazz started out as the articulation of that same feeling, and ingenious approximation of the human voice.
>
> *Feel Like Going Home*
> by Peter Guralnick

Recalling his youthful days working in the fields near Clarksdale, Mississippi, Muddy Waters told Paul Oliver about the daily routine of back-breaking labor during the Great Depression: "Every man would be hollerin' in the fields but you didn't pay that no mind. Yeah, of course, I'd holler too. You might call them blues but they was just made up things. . . .I was always singing just the way I felt."

Although Muddy said that just about everybody "could play some kind of instrument during those days," it was in the fields that hollers and chants gave expression to the most basic form of the blues. These work songs were perhaps the most powerful of all the blues—a spontaneous, heart-rending expression of the moment. They expressed grief, misery, anxiety, and pain, as well as happiness or delight. The form allowed any type of emotion to come through. Sung rhythmically, the songs helped the work by setting a pace for the endlessly tedious hours of labor. The 'call and response' form, in which a leader sings a verse and a group sings a chorus in return, may explain in part the role of the guitar in more modern blues. As LeRoi Jones writes in his compelling book *Blues People*: "Blues playing is the closest imitation of the human voice of any music I've heard; the vocal effects that jazz musicians have delighted in from Bunk Johnson to Ornette Coleman are evidence of this."

A standard call and response verse, such as

> *Gonna shout trouble over*
> *When I get home*
> *Gonna meet my maker*
> *When I get home*

set up a repetitive structure that can be found in blues to this day. Rather than have a vocal chorus answer a lead singer, guitar riffs were used to respond, filling in spaces between verses, adding texture to the material. This became particularly apparent in Chicago blues where the electric guitar consistently echoed the lead singer's verses.

Riffs are used in three basic ways: to mimic the vocalist in the call and response manner we have discussed, to play turnarounds that bring the tune from the end of one verse to the beginning of the next, and as thematic lines that help to structure a song. In the following pages, we will take a look at some of stylistic variations in riffs performed by Chicago blues guitarists. Played at their best, they form a perfect complement to the singer's voice, a fluid extension of a vocal idea.

EARL HOOKER

Earl Hooker, originally born in Clarksdale, Mississippi in 1930, moved to the Windy City when he was just a year old. He began playing guitar in 1945, learning quickly enough to play with such legendary artists as Junior Wells, Muddy Waters, and Ike Turner by the early fifties. Hooker is an extremely versatile musician who knows his way around jazz, R&B, and even country-and-western styles of guitar playing. In a conversation with record producer Chris Strachwitz after recording his Arhoolie album *Two Bugs and a Roach* (F 1044), Earl Hooker described his unexpected entry into the world of country music:

"I went to Waterloo, Iowa—went to a joint where some hillbilly boys were playing—I asked the guy to let me sit in. Everybody was looking at me—they said this is something they got to dig—a colored guy playing hillbilly music, in a hillbilly joint! I went to play my guitar, doing 'Walking the Floor over You' and 'Your Cheating Heart.'"

Apparently the musicians and the audience loved Hooker's style. He got a job playing in the house band for six months.

Our first example of Earl Hooker's playing is certainly a far cry from country-and-western—it is a straight-out, funky blues idea from his song "Two Bugs and a Roach." This is a good example of a guitar bass-line, played with a rhythm part, setting the theme for a tune.

44

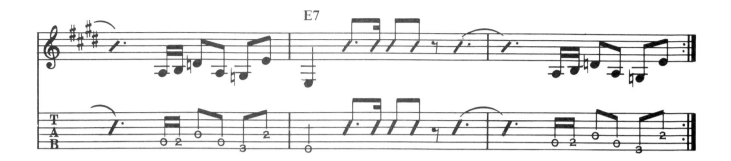

The second example is from Hooker's slide guitar playing as played on a tune called "Anna Lee." The first lick is a typical Hooker opening coming out of the V chord, in this case a B7.

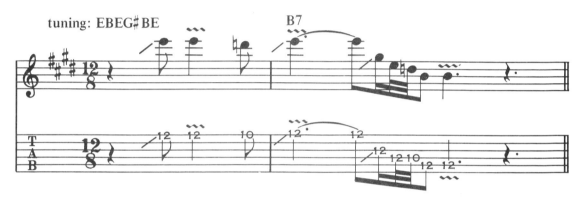

The next lick is a repetitious lick played on an A7 chord. It is a device, as is the one that follows, which repeats the B note five times. Earl Hooker had a powerful influence on Jeff Beck's slide playing, particularly in his use of vibrato.

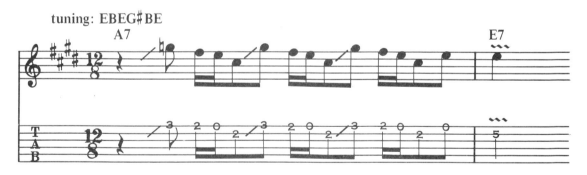

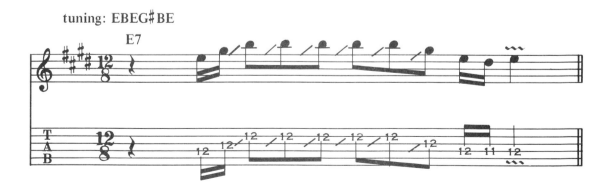

SON SEALS

Son Seals is a clean, emotional guitarist, whose performances have the signature of a true craftsman about them. He is considered, as writer Bruce Iglauer notes, "one of a whole new generation of black blues musicians, a generation hidden in the big city ghettos and the small towns of the deep South." Seals was born in Osceola, Arkansas in 1942, a town that also claims Albert King (born Albert Nelson) as its own. As a youngster, Seals confessed to Peter Guralnick: "Music was all I could think of. I was in a sense luckier than the average kid, growing up in that kind of environment. I wanted to play so bad I could taste it."

Son Seals began his career as a drummer, performing behind local bluesmen before starting his own band, the Upsetters. Eventually, he joined up with Albert King, playing drums at first and later guitar. He can be heard on King's *Live Wire/Blues Power* album, and as Guralnick noted in *Lost Highway*: "There is no question of Albert's style upon Son's work—his thick-toned, heavily amplified, dirty-sounding guitar owes a debt to King in particular that many of Son's contemporaries share."

Seals acknowledges his debt to Albert King, but added, in a conversation with journalist Jerry De Muth in 1973: "I try to play my own style too. I always liked B.B. King and Albert King. I can play like Albert, but I feel it don't really accomplish anything. If you do your *own stuff*, create it yourself, you know you are deep down in it."

Our first Son Seals example is from "Cotton Pickin' Blues" (Alligator 4703) and is a lick that sets up the vocal line that follows immediately. In this case, it is also played in unison by the organ and the bass.

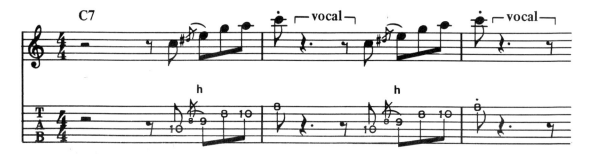

The following examples give a sense of Son Seal's basic approach to playing solos, and are taken from his tune "Going Home Tomorrow."

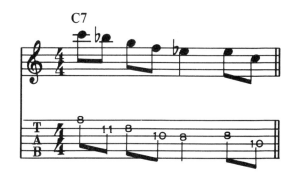

HOWLIN' WOLF/HUBERT SUMLIN

Chester Arthur Burnett, aka Howlin' Wolf, was born in 1910 in a farm area near Ruleville, Mississippi. He told writer Arnold Shaw in the classic study *Honkers and Shouters* that he had spent his early years "working on the farm with my father, baling hay and driving tractors, fixing fences, pickin' cotton and pullin' corn. . . .There was a lot of music around there. Work songs. They'd get me out there and sing as they work—plowing songs, songs to call mules by. . . ." When Wolf was eighteen years old his father bought him a guitar. Charley Patton became Wolf's first teacher. "Patton started me off playing," Wolf told writer Pete Welding. "He showed me things on the guitar. . . .I also heard records by Lonnie Johnson, Tampa Red, and Blind Blake." Arnold Shaw points out that the Wolf's strangest influence was "the white blues yodeler Jimmie Rogers, the Singing Brakeman, . . .who is recognized as the 'Father of Country Music.' "

"I couldn't do no yodeling," the Wolf said. "So I turned to growlin', and the howlin', and it's done me just fine." Howlin' Wolf moved to Chicago in 1952, already a fully developed blues performer leading his own electric band. Muddy Waters helped him get his first Chicago gig, despite a personal rivalry that flared between them in subsequent years. Chess records signed Wolf to cut some sides, and it was for these sessions that guitarist Hubert Sumlin came from Mississippi to Chicago. Sumlin's raspy, down-home brilliance became a vital part of Howlin' Wolf's sound, and to an extent the two seem interchangable on those early Chess recordings. Sumlin's guitar, occasionally doubling Wolf's hamonica playing, make those early records of "Little Red Rooster," "Smokestack Lightning," and others almost unbearably exciting. They invoked the darkly ambient flavor of the city, recalling late nights in smoky, neon-lit South Side bars and the tension of Chicago's tough underside.

Hubert Sumlin was just fourteen years old when he saw Howlin' Wolf for the first time in 1948. Sumlin was a plantation worker in Mississippi at the time.

"I got interested in music," he told Peter Guralnick. "She [Sumlin's mother] bought me a ten dollar guitar just like the kind Wolf has, a round hole guitar. . . .I took it with me into the field. The man caught me, she-it, it was me and his son, he broke it right across the tractor wheel. Well, after that he bought me a twenty dollar guitar."

Wolf was playing at Silkhairs, a popular local club, and Sumlin, being underage, had to sneak in to listen. "I went and played every night. And then I got hired. It took me two months to get hired. But I kept going every night. And I been with him ever since."

Sumlin is probably the only musician to stay with the Wolf for a long period of time, and Guralnick describes their friendship as "locked forever in a love-hate, affection-spite, typical father and son relationship. Perhaps it is this closeness that made their music so sympathetic, so hard to separate."

Howlin' Wolf died on January 10, 1976, in Chicago.

Following is a typical bass lick as used by Wolf and Sumlin to set the tone for a song, in this case "Miss James."

Here is the bass line from "Born under a Bad Sign."

OTIS RUSH

The first time I heard Otis Rush, in a small Greenwich Village nightclub in the late sixties, I was completely knocked out. He seemed to play with a grace and style that was different from other blues guitarists. He was smooth, dashing off ornate riffs with an easy, almost detached style. Coming to New York as a virtual unknown, he captured the imaginations of aspiring local guitarists overnight and front-row seats were reserved by Jimi Hendrix and Michael Bloomfield among others.

Part of Otis Rush's appeal at the time was his youthful approach to the guitar. In 1969, Rush was only thirty-five years old. Completely aware of contemporary trends in popular music and culture, yet deeply mired in the tradition of the older generation of bluesmen, Rush claimed Muddy Waters, Little Walter, and John Lee Hooker as influences. Born in 1934 in Mississippi, Rush moved to Chicago in 1949 where he quickly won the respect of established local performers. His recording career, a series of contractual hassles and plain bad luck, has prevented him (so far) from reaching the audience he so well deserves. Still, what little there is on vinyl is as good as any blues available. We recommend the Bullfrog LP *Right Place, Wrong Time* (301) which was coproduced by Nick Gravenites.

We have chosen five licks from a tune called "Tore Up" that are quite typical of Otis Rush's style. The notes are not particularly difficult here—what really matters is the way Rush himself played them; that is, with exceptional ease and grace.

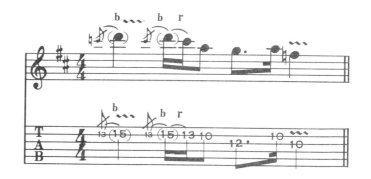

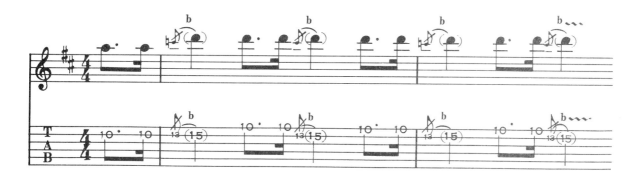

49

ELMORE JAMES

Elmore James is one of those blues guitarists that almost everyone in Chicago cites as an influence. When he arrived there in 1953, he quickly settled into a community full of musicians with roots in his native Mississippi, where he was born in 1918. James was a great fan of Robert Johnson's powerful acoustic guitar style, particularly Johnson's bottleneck material. In Chicago Elmore James adapted his style to electric ensemble playing and became famous throughout the area. His early recordings with the Broomdusters in the 1950s became legendary, and over the years he cut sides with many different labels, including Chief, Vee Jay, Fire, and Chess.

Arnold Shaw quotes guitarist J.B. Hutto telling of James's influence on him: "One night I heard Elmore James. He played it different from anybody. Old bottleneck guitar had died out by then. And Elmore was the first I ever heard go at an electric guitar with a bar. Well, I never heard anything like that before. So I got me a guitar and a piece of pipe and I went to work with the two of them."

Our Elmore James example, from his tune "Talk to Me Baby" (Chess 1537) is in open-D tuning, and is played in his slide style.

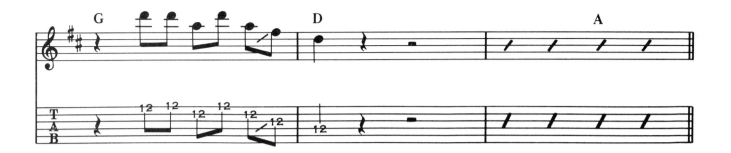

HOUND DOG TAYLOR

Hound Dog Taylor, born as Theodore Roosevelt Taylor in 1915 in Natchez, Mississippi, has been a fixture around Chicago's South Side clubs for quite a while now. As a friend of Elmore James, Hound Dog developed a raspy, funky, down-home style with a bottleneck approach. Taylor came to Chicago in 1942 but it wasn't until 1957 that he became a professional musician. His raw, unadulterated sound has made him almost legendary on the Chicago scene while he remains virtually unknown on the national level.

We have chosen to illustrate his style with the blues classic "It Hurts Me Too," as recorded on his Alligator album, *Hound Dog Taylor and the Houserockers* (4701). One interesting point about this recording is that Hound Dog uses two guitars and drums only. The guitars are plugged directly into a tape recorder and the distorted sound comes from overloading the input volume of the tape deck itself. The following examples are in open-E tuning and are played with a slide.

ALBERT KING

In our opinion, Albert King is probably the most remarkable blues guitarist of his era, responsible for creating a unique sound as well as a host of imaginative riffs. The left-handed guitarist from Indianola, Mississippi began his career in the late 1940s with the Harmony Kings, a gospel group. In Chicago, he played drums with Jimmy Reed before breaking out on his own with an album for Parrot Records in 1953. Over the years Albert King worked with such stars as Brook Benton and Jackie Wilson and came into his own as a guitarist during the fifties and sixties. In 1969, after receiving exceptional national notices for his albums on Stax Records, King finally hit his stride.

"My days of paying dues are over," he said. "Now it's my time to do the collecting."

All of the following examples are played with the side of the right-hand thumb. The bends must be executed precisely, occasionally spanning a full major 3rd. The first example is from the song "Born under a Bad Sign" and shows the use of the bass line to set up a tune.

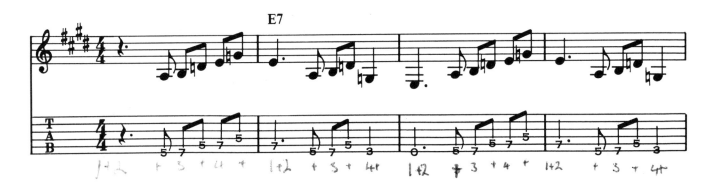

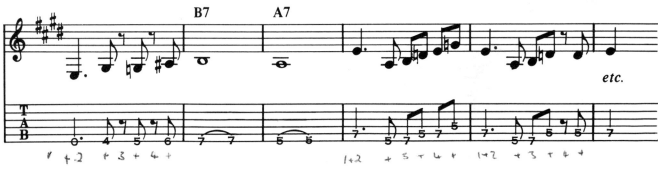

The next three licks are taken from King's tune "Searching for a Woman" (Chess 1538).

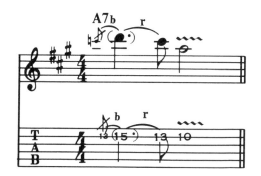

Here are a few from "Can't Stop Hangin' 'Round." They give you a good idea of the range of Albert King's style.

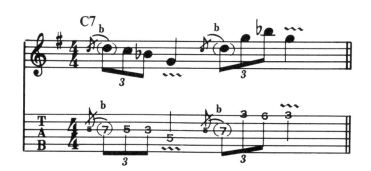

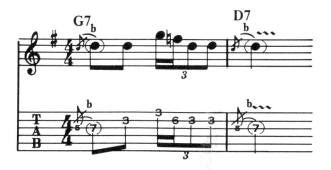

(For more on Albert King's style, as well as three transcribed solos, see the section *Albert King* following.)

B.B. KING

A great deal has been written about B.B. King who is by far the most famous of the Chicago blues guitarists. King was also born in Indianola, Mississippi, in 1925, as Riley B. King. Originally influenced by country bluesmen Blind Lemon Jefferson, Sonny Boy Williamson, and Bukka White, B.B. King later became interested in jazz musicians like Charlie Christian, Django Reinhardt, and T-Bone Walker, among many others. The striking quality of B.B. King, as Arnold Shaw points out, is that he "has never stopped growing or seeking new musical worlds to conquer, but he integrates what he learns into the framework of his basic orientation as a bluesman."

In the following examples, B.B. King uses a *staccato* style that he has developed during the past few years. He tends to muffle notes (intentionally) at the end of phrases instead of letting them ring out as he did in the past. For reference, check B.B. King's *Alive and Well* album (Bluesway 6031), where he first introduced this technique.

We will begin our examples with a guitar-bass riff from his tune "No Good."

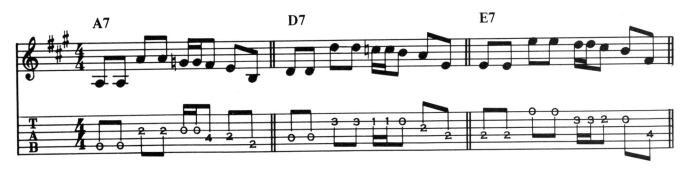

The next bunch are taken from the same recording and demonstrate B.B.'s approach to playing, if only a small part of his immense catalogue of ideas.

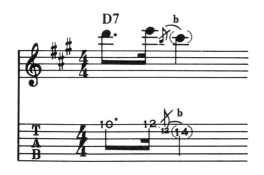
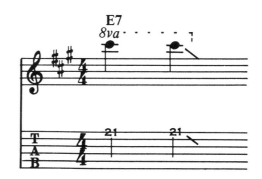

As Mike Bloomfield once said, "I come from B.B. King." This is a statement, critic Ralph Gleason once noted, that any rock or blues guitarist will undoubtedly aver. B.B. King's influence is everywhere.

(For more on B.B. King see the section *B.B. King* following.)

Albert King

ALBERT KING

> Born under a bad sign;
> Been down since I began to crawl.
> If it wasn't for bad luck
> I wouldn't have no luck at all.
> "Born under a Bad Sign"
> by Booker T. Jones and William Bell

Albert King once explained to Dan Forte of *Guitar Player* magazine that "I never could hold a pick in my hand. I started out playing with one, but I'd really be gettin' into it, and after a while the pick would sail across the house. I said to hell with this. So I just play with the meat of the thumb." Somehow he still manages to get a percussive, biting sound from his instrument which complements perfectly the unique horn arrangements on his recordings. We have taken ideas from a batch of wonderful King albums. All of them are highly recommended listening; especiallly *The Big Blues* (King 1060) and *Born under a Bad Sign* (Stax S723).

Albert King has a basic vocabulary of riffs from which he creates his solos. Although we have presented several in the preceding chapter, we have decided to include some more because they can be played out of context and still remain gems of blues guitar.

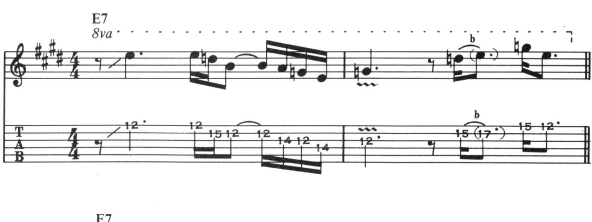

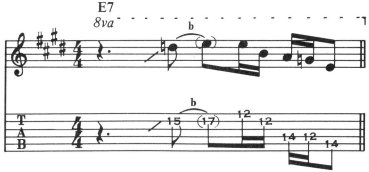

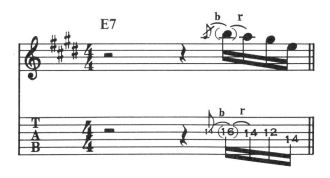

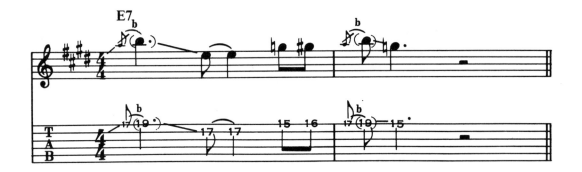

The following solos are complicated and tricky, but they can be mastered if you begin studying them at a slow tempo. It's best to listen to his recordings in order to really understand his sense of phrasing and dynamics.

Walked All Night Long

With a swing
Intro

Hound Dog Taylor

Natural Ball

Crosscut Saw

MUDDY WATERS

> Muddy Waters, who was completely dominated by Robert Johnson's recordings in the late thirties, learned the technique from Son House, who had taught the same things to Robert several years before. It was Robert's style that excited Muddy. When Muddy Waters started his first bands in Chicago...all he had to do was have the bass player and drummer pick up on the bass part of Robert's style, and let the harmonica and the lead guitar pick up on the treble.
>
> *Robert Johnson* by Sam Charters

McKinley Morganfield claims that he got his nickname because "I was always playin' in the creek and gettin' dirty and my sisters called me Muddy Waters then." The name stuck with him well after he left Mississippi and followed him to Chicago. It wasn't until 1947 that Muddy Waters got his first break in the Windy City. According to Arnold Shaw, it was Big Bill Broonzy, the famous acoustic bluesman who "presented Muddy at Sylvio's, the club at West Lake and persuaded Mayo Williams to produced some records with him on Columbia." Up until that time, Muddy's only recordings were done on acoustic guitar for the Library of Congress in 1942. These recordings (rereleased by Testament Records, T2210) clearly show the influence of Son House and Robert Johnson, two players revered by Muddy while he was learning to play in Mississippi. "Of course there was Robert Johnson," Muddy told Paul Oliver, "he used to work the jukes. He was the kind of guy you wanted to listen to, get ideas from." Pete Welding points out Johnson's influence on specific selections. "I Be's Trouble," "You Got to Take Sick," "Country Blues," and others, show Muddy "completely in the sway of Johnson's compelling music." His bottleneck technique was taught to him by "Sonny House—the best we had. He used to have a neck of a bottle over his finger, little finger, touch the strings with that and make them sing." These early recordings show Muddy Waters to be a master of country-style bottleneck guitar, but he was also destined to become one of the great Chicago-style slide players.

Muddy Waters recorded several sides for the Aristocrat label between 1947 and 1951. These cuts are known as the first publicly released Chicago blues. Soon afterward, Waters released "Louisiana Blues" and "Rolling Stone" for Chess Records which brought him some national recognition. These semi-hits allowed Muddy Waters to form his own bands, and work with some of the finest blues players of the time: James Cotton on harp, Otis Spann on piano, Buddy Guy on rhythm guitar, and Willie Dixon on bass. Paul Oliver described a performance given by Muddy: "There was no doubting who was king—the effect was stunning. And frightening too. The sheer physical drive of band and blues singer chilled the spine. Muddy roared, leaped, jerked in fierce and violent spasms. When he came off the stage, he was in a state of near trance and the sweat poured off him."

We have chosen this slide example from an album organized by Mike Bloomfield (former lead guitarist with the Paul Butterfield Blues Band) called *Fathers and Sons*. It's an excellent example of Muddy's fluid, smooth, slide technique and uses elements from his past and present styles.

Muddy Waters

Long Distance Call

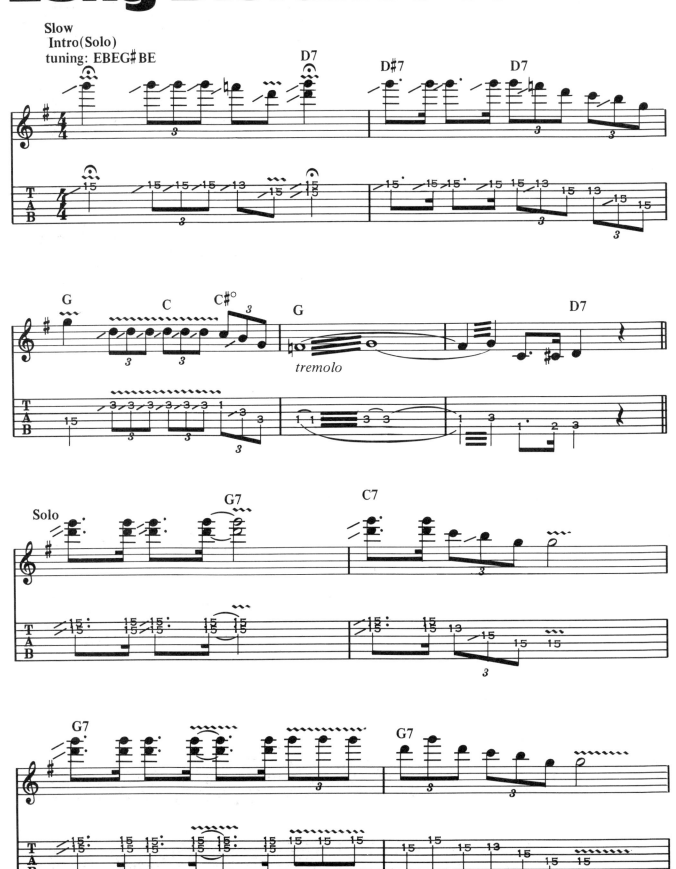

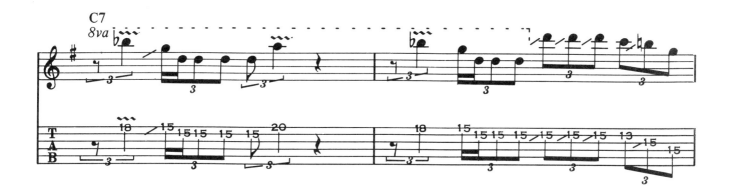
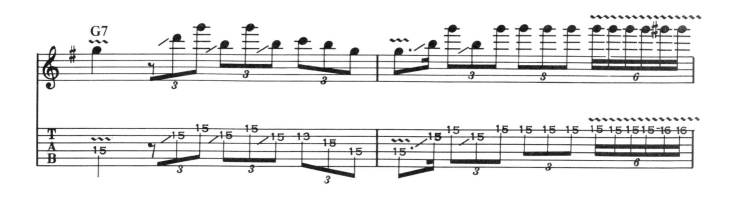

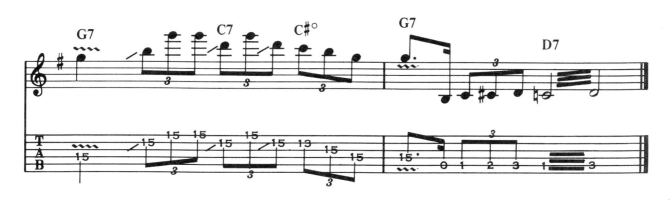

71

Buddy Guy

BUDDY GUY

Robert Johnson influenced Elmore James and Muddy Waters; and they in turn, influenced Buddy Guy. While he is considered one of the younger bluesmen to come out of the Chicago scene, his playing has a mature, sophisticated quality to it. Buddy Guy was brought up in Baton Rouge, Louisiana, but moved to Chicago where he has worked in numerous blues bands, including those of Muddy Waters and Junior Wells. He plays a Fender *Stratocaster*, which gives him a crisp, tight-sounding tone, and you can hear many threads of influences weave through his own unique style. We have chosen two solos from his solo album *A Man and the Blues* (Vanguard 79272) to represent him.

A Man and the Blues

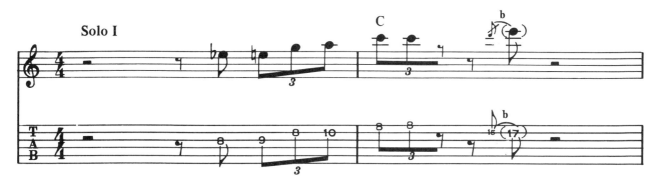

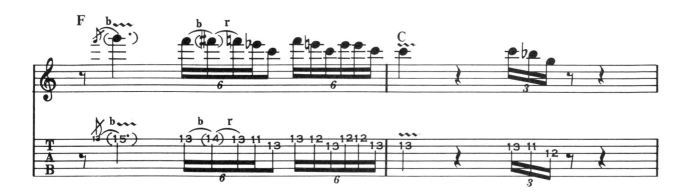

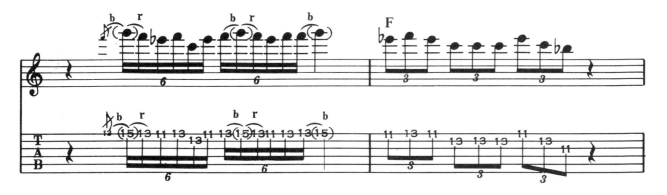

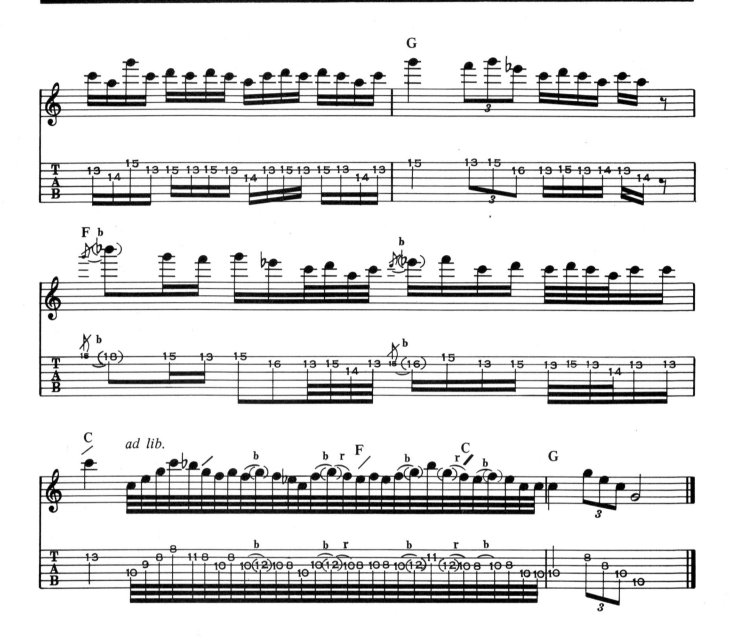

Buddy Guy and Junior Wells

Mary Had a Little Lamb

FREDDIE KING

Freddie King's style has come a long way from his somewhat cute and commercial early hits "Hide Away" and "San-Ho-Zay"; to his down-home versions of "I'm Going Down" or "Dust My Blues." We like both styles equally well, but it almost seems like some of the earlier tunes were prepackaged by King records who gave his albums such names as *Freddie King Goes Surfin'* or *Let's Hide Away and Dance Away with Freddie King*. Fortunately, "Hide Away" became a smash single in 1961 and put Freddie King on the national touring circuit. Guitarist Luther Tucker, who worked with James Cotton and Little Walter before starting his own band, recalls jamming with Magic Sam, Otis Rush, and Freddie King: "Seems like didn't a week go by," he told Joel Selvin in *Guitar Player*, "when all four of us be at one club jamming together on stage all night. I remember Magic Sam and Freddie King bopping heads over 'Hide Away.' They had different ideas about who would cut it. Finally, Sam heard it on a jukebox one night and found out Freddie had beat him to it."

Freddie King's version of "Dust My Broom" is fascinating because he plays it on acoustic guitar. Freddie King might be the only player transcribed in this book who wasn't born in Mississippi, but in Gilmer, Texas in 1934. Like his fellow bluesmen he was brought up listening to the likes of T-Bone Walker, John Lee Hooker, and Muddy Waters. He started playing at the tender age of six, learning from his uncle and mother on an acoustic Silvertone guitar. Freddie plays with his fingers, and learned to use fingerpicks from Eddie Taylor and Jimmy Rogers after he moved to Chicago in the early 1950s. "Actually," he said, "I used the picks to save my fingers. I pick real hard and my fingers would get sore." Although he used to play Fender guitars, Freddie King now plays a stereo Gibson *ES 335*, explaining that "for the way I play, I think Gibson is the best."

Freddy King, Walton's corner

Dust My Broom

Elmore James

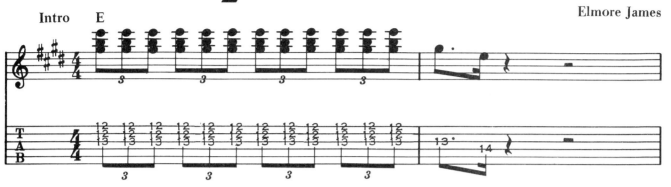
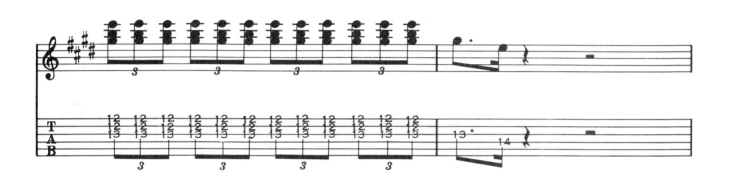

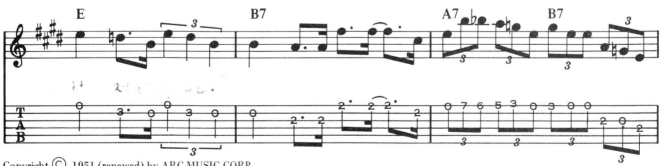

Copyright © 1951 (renewed) by ARC MUSIC CORP.,
New York, N.Y. International Copyright Secured.
All Rights Reserved. Used By Permission.

I'm Goin' Down

Don Nix

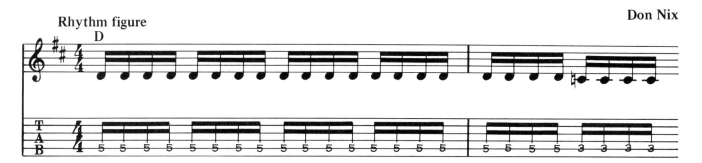
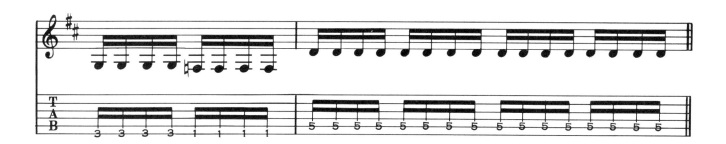
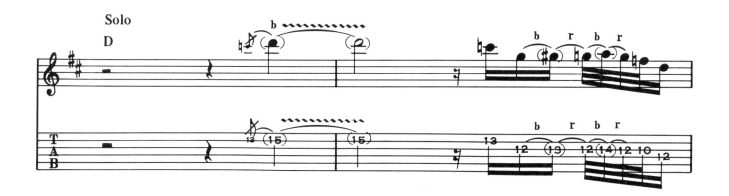
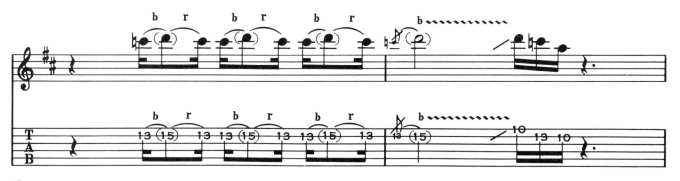

© 1969 Irving Music, Inc.
All Rights Reserved. International
Copyright Secured. Used By Permission.

Following are three solos that we have created to represent the popular, funky style associated with Freddie in the early sixties.

Hidden Away

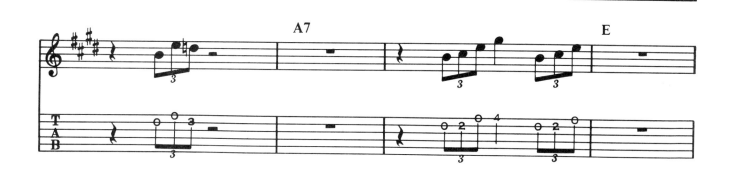

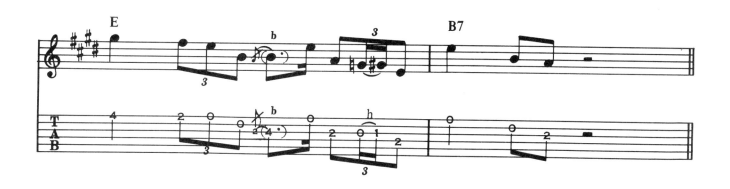

Accompanying bass figure for "Hidden Away"

Elmore James and unidentified woman

Swishy

San-Dee-Ay-Go

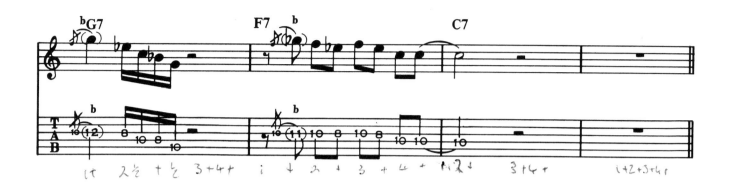

Accompanying bass figure for "San-Dee-Ay-Go" (this can be played through all the changes).

91

B.B. KING

> You either change with the times or you find yourself looking at empty seats.
>
> B.B. King to Arnold Shaw

B.B. King is certainly the most famous blues guitarist to come out of Chicago and he may be the most sophisticated as well. In Mississippi he was exposed to the raw, natural blues that continues to be a part of his style, but he was strongly influenced by Django Reinhardt, T-Bone Walker, Charlie Christian, Count Basie, Duke Ellington, Lowell Fulson, Joe Turner, Lightnin' Hopkins, and many others. He is a slick, professional entertainer, who has recorded countless sides for many labels.

We have created the following tune to show you how B.B. might solo over a standard, minor blues progression.

B.B. King

I Lost My Thrill

DISCOGRAPHY

Freddie King Sings KING 762
My Feeling for the Blues Freddie King COTILLION SD 9016
Freddie King Goes Surfin' KING 856
Getting Ready Freddie King SHELTER 8905
I'm Jimmy Reed VEE JAY 1004
Otis Rush, Right Place BULLFROG 301
Howlin' Wolf CHESS 1502
A Message to the Young Howlin' Wolf CHESS 50002
T-Bone Blues ATLANTIC 8256
Live and Well B.B. King BLUESWAY 6031
Muddy Waters—Down on Stovall's Plantation TESTAMENT T 2210
Door to Door Albert King and Otis Rush CHESS 1538
King of Blues Guitar Albert King ATLANTIC SD Z3213
Singin' the Blues B.B. King UNITED 7726
Whose Muddy Shoes Elmore James and John Brim CHESS 1537
A Man and the Blues Buddy Guy VANGUARD VSD 79272
Things I Used to Do Pee Wee Crayton VANGUARD VSD 6566
Nothing but the Blues (Anthology) CBS 66278

Maxwell Street, Chicago

BIBLIOGRAPHY

Many books have been invaluable aids to the gathering of information for this book. The following list represents some of the best and most readable.

Honkers and Shouters: The Golden Years of R&B, by Arnold Shaw, Collier Books, 1978.
> This is an informal history of the musicians, record companies, and social forces responsible for the rise of rhythm and blues over the past few decades. A mammoth amount of research went into this work, and its fast, entertaining text is both detailed and accurate. A must-read for blues fans!

The Story of the Blues, by Paul Oliver, Chilton Books, 1969.
> A detailed social history of the blues from its origins to the present. Very good on country blues musicians and full of wonderful illustrations.

Robert Johnson, by Sam Charters, Oak Publications, 1973.
> An excellent tapestry about the legendary bluesman woven from sparse threads of information about his life and from his songs (music and lyrics included).

The Legacy of the Blues, by Sam Charters, Da Capo Press, 1977.
> Personal close-ups on the lives and struggles of twelve bluesmen.

Lost Highway, by Peter Guralnick, Godine Books, 1979.
> This book is a highly moving study of American musicians written with respect and sensitivity by an excellent critic.

Almost every issue of *Guitar Player* magazine features stories on blues guitarists. For that and many other reasons we can't recommend too highly reading it regularly. The specific issues and articles that we've used in researching this book are:

October, 1970; "Bo Diddley"
December, 1973; "Luther Tucker"
January, 1977; "Freddie King"
December 1977; "Les Paul"